T0383475

Bogdanović
by
Bogdanović

Yugoslav Memorials
through the
Eyes of Their Architect

Edited by
Vladimir Kulić

The Museum of Modern Art
New York

Foreword

Bogdanović by Bogdanović presents a suite of captivating photographs taken by the late Yugoslav architect, writer, and politician Bogdan Bogdanović of a select number of the many monuments and sites of commemoration he designed. Born in 1922 in Belgrade, into a cosmopolitan family with ties to the local Surrealist circles, Bogdanović studied architecture in his hometown and would rise to become one of the most important architects and public intellectuals in socialist Yugoslavia. Parallel to international currents of postmodern critique, Bogdanović also made a name for himself as an early and outspoken critic of those tendencies in postwar architecture culture that privileged technocratic and functionalist problem-solving over the creation of memorable spaces in the service of society.

Bogdanović's many monuments, which were built throughout the culturally and topographically diverse territory of the former Yugoslavia, manifest a poetic sensibility. Given his background, Bogdanović's work has often been characterized as a Surrealist architecture, and indeed his plastically articulate structures conjure with uncanny power strong yet oneiric images. Usually embedded in large-scale parklike settings, Bogdanović's monuments are as much stunning objects as they are landscapes of experience that transform the passive visitor into an engaged participant in the act of contemplative commemoration. Like the monuments themselves, Bogdanović's idiosyncratic photographic interpretations of his built work convey a sense of the dreamlike—and elicit a visceral response to the calamitous loss of human life that these monuments commemorate.

A few of Bogdanović's monuments have received a great deal of attention in recent years on various social media platforms, where they have, through ignorance, often been branded as "Soviet" or "Communist," when their primary purpose was to memorialize the victims of fascism, the sites of concentration camps, and various atrocities of World War II—their unifying program of collective recollection of shared trauma, heroism, and perseverance serving the ideological and social aims of the newly founded Yugoslav state. By once again giving voice to the author of these powerful creations, this book is intended to recover the original memorial function of these structures and their role in fostering a vibrant, multiethnic society.

Bogdanović by Bogdanović is the result of Vladimir Kulić and Wolfgang Thaler's research into Bogdanović's private photo archive. We are thankful to Vladimir for having brought this visual trove to our attention as we worked together organizing the exhibition (July 15, 2018–January 13, 2019) and editing the book *Toward a Concrete Utopia: Architecture in Yugoslavia, 1948–1980*. Like the latter, the present volume attempts to position Bogdanović's legacy in various contexts. While the society in and for which these works were originally conceived no longer exists, *Bogdanović by Bogdanović* is a striking illustration of their ongoing historical and aesthetic relevance.

MARTINO STIERLI
The Philip Johnson Chief Curator
of Architecture and Design
The Museum of Modern Art

The Life and Work of Bogdan Bogdanović: An Introduction

Vladimir Kulić

Between 1951 and 1987, the architect Bogdan Bogdanović built more than twenty monuments, cemeteries, mausoleums, memorial parks, necropolises, cenotaphs, and other sites of memory. They are scattered throughout the former Yugoslavia, in what is present-day Bosnia and Herzegovina, Croatia, Kosovo, Macedonia, Montenegro, and Serbia. (Slovenia is the only region of the former Yugoslavia in which Bogdanović never built a memorial.) Varying in shape, size, and location, these memorials all departed from the conventions of commemorative art to reinvent its terms in the wake of World War II. Rejecting both the waning realism and the ascendant abstraction of the day, Bogdanović drew on his formative experiences in Surrealism and on his erudite knowledge of architectural history and anthropology to inject commemoration with a new life. At a time when most European architects, both in the socialist East and the capitalist West, optimistically embraced modernist forms as the language of postwar reconstruction and modernization, Bogdanović relied on allusive organic shapes, ambiguous historical references, extensive earthworks, and an abundance of ornament to produce one of the most idiosyncratic architectural oeuvres of the postwar era.

Bogdanović's memorials are among the central achievements of the commemorative art of socialist Yugoslavia. In recent years, mesmerizing images of Yugoslav monuments have attracted broad attention in the digital realm—whether on major news outlets or anonymous blogs or via endless sharing on social media. Such rediscovery suggests that this otherwise little-known body of postwar art deserves broader attention; unfortunately, the information circulating in the media is generally lacking and often outright erroneous, rarely concerned with the history behind these monuments or with the artists who created them. All we see are massive, anonymous shapes constructed out of reinforced concrete or steel, standing desolate and mute amid unfamiliar landscapes.

This book offers more nuanced insight into Yugoslav memorials. It focuses on one of their most important creators, who remains widely known in the region, as well as in Austria, where he spent the last sixteen years of his life, exiled for his opposition to the nationalist rule of Slobodan Milošević. Outside of Central Europe, however, he is far less recognized. The present volume allows us to see his oeuvre through his own eyes, or more precisely, through the lens of his camera. For Bogdanović was not only a celebrated architect, an influential urban theorist, a charismatic professor at the University of Belgrade, a public intellectual, and a one-time mayor of Belgrade—he was also a passionate photographer. Beginning in the early 1960s, when he spent the entire honorarium for one of his projects to purchase a professional medium-format camera, he made an effort to photograph his built work. The result is a collection of photos that document his memorials at the time of their completion, before the patina of time, neglect, and deliberate human aggression began to chip away at them. Carefully staged, attentive to focus, framing, and lighting, they are in themselves works of art. Very few have ever been published. The pictures are part of a broader body of work Bogdanović kept largely private, which, in addition to many more images of memorials, also includes various experiments with photographic techniques and subject matter. This book makes some of these photos available for the first time as a collection, accompanied by Bogdanović's own words, recorded over a series of conversations with me in 2005.

•••

Bogdan Bogdanović (1922–2010) was born in Belgrade, then in the Kingdom of Serbs, Croats, and Slovenes (later the Kingdom of Yugoslavia), son of the prominent literary critic Milan Bogdanović. His family was left-leaning and decidedly antimonarchist; nevertheless, young Bogdan was at one moment recruited to play with the crown prince, Peter, soon to become the last king of Yugoslavia. Bogdanović grew up surrounded by the progressive cultural elite of the country; among the many prominent figures with which the family socialized were the famous writer Miroslav Krleža and the leading modernist architects Nikola Dobrović and Drago Ibler. However, as early as Bogdanović's teenage years, the most decisive influence for his intellectual development was Marko Ristić, leader of the Belgrade Surrealist group. The circle around Ristić was one of the earliest and most prolific offshoots of the international Surrealist movement. Cosmopolitan and widely educated, in direct contact with André Breton and the Centrale Surréaliste in Paris, Belgrade Surrealists were politically even more radical than their French peers.[1] Devoted to the Marxist cause and allied with the illegal Communist Party of Yugoslavia, they did not shy away from controversy, opposing the official party line and its cultural policy based on Soviet-style Socialist Realism, which became obligatory after Stalin solidified his power in the 1930s.[2] Bogdanović's formative years thus combined firsthand indoctrination in Surrealism and Marxism, as well as a certain nonconformism, all of which would set the course of his aesthetic and political engagement for the rest of his life.

Bogdanović enrolled at the University of Belgrade in the fall of 1940, but his studies of architecture were cut short the following spring by the occupation and partitioning of Yugoslavia by the Axis forces. He spent most of the war in the city, in contact with the Communist resistance. These desolate years were not entirely lost for his architectural edification: during that time, Bogdanović dove into architectural history, discovering the work of great classicist architects such as Claude-Nicolas Ledoux and Karl Friedrich Schinkel, as well as of his own contemporary Jože Plečnik, whose free treatment of the classical tradition became another formative influence. In the spring of 1944 Bogdanović escaped Belgrade to join the Communist-led People's Liberation Movement, where he quickly

FIG. 1. HOUSING FOR THE STAFF OF THE JAROSLAV ČERNI HYDROTECHNICAL INSTITUTE, OUTSIDE OF BELGRADE, SERBIA. 1952–53

rose in the ranks, joined the Communist Party of Yugoslavia, and was badly wounded in combat. He returned from the war with the prestige of having been a part of the liberation movement, which propelled his professional ambitions for the rest of his career.

After reenrolling at the university, Bogdanović graduated with a degree in architecture in 1950 and immediately got a teaching position in the Department of Urban Planning. Disheartened by the extreme austerity of contemporary architectural production, he found refuge in writing. His first book, *Small Urbanism* (1958), is a collection of essays he had published in various periodicals, in which he critiques the overt rationalism of postwar reconstruction and draws attention to the human scale of urban life. The book installed Bogdanović as an important voice in Yugoslav architecture, and his influence only grew over the next thirty years with a steady flow of books and articles, predominantly devoted to the history and meaning of the city.[3] Drawing on a wide range of sources—from anthropology and classical mythology to psychology and game theory—Bogdanović called for a rehumanization of the modern metropolis, stressing the significance of its deeply meaningful, socially constructed nature. Equally influential among his writings, albeit rather different in genre, was *The Futile Trowel: The Doctrine and Practice of the Brotherhood of Golden (Black) Numbers* (1963). Oscillating between a Surrealist phantasmagoria and a quasi-scholarly treatise, this volume described the author's imagined

induction into the brotherhood of great architects, which included Bramante, Palladio, Borromini, Guarini, Piranesi, Ledoux, and Gaudí.[4] *The Futile Trowel* was a cult text for generations of architecture students in Yugoslavia, introducing an unlikely set of heroes and values at a time when high modernism dominated everyday production.

Even though he refused to conform to the prevailing modernist orthodoxy, Bogdanović sought to pursue a conventional architectural career throughout the 1950s via projects that ranged from urban plans for provincial towns to housing and office-building designs. However, most of this work remained unrealized. A rare exception was a group of houses for the employees of the Jaroslav Černi Hydrotechnical Institute (fig. 1), built in 1952 and 1953 at the foot of Mount Avala on the outskirts of Belgrade. Although very modest in material and size, the project was nevertheless unusual for the time in its exaggerated signifiers of traditional domesticity: gabled fronts of rustic stone, outsize window frames, and massive brick chimneys projecting from the facades. Despite the symmetry of the pitched roofs, the composition of the gabled facades placed their various elements—the windows, the shifting plane of the wall—in deliberate contradiction to each other, perhaps anticipating subsequent postmodernist strategies.[5] Almost a decade later, the remodel of the nineteenth-century Villa of Queen Natalija (1961) in Smederevo, Serbia, similarly foreshadowed postmodernist themes: a deliberate

9

homage to neo-Palladian architecture, it nevertheless interpreted its sources in a deliberately ironic way, employing improbably thin columns made from plumbing pipes and classical ornaments flattened out and transformed into simple signs. The villa was the last conventional piece of architecture Bogdanović would ever complete; his career as a memorial builder was taking off.

In retrospect, Bogdanović's very first built work appears prophetic for the rest of his working life, even though it took a while for the project's promise to materialize. A short time after graduating, he was invited to submit a proposal in a competition organized by the Jewish community of Belgrade for the Monument to the Jewish Victims of Fascism at the local Sephardic cemetery (fig. 2). The seven invited architects included Bogdanović's university peer Aljoša (Alexis) Josić, later of the famous French office Candilis-Josic-Woods.[6] Bogdanović won the competition and constructed the monument in 1951 and 1952, producing a formally simple yet symbolically multivalent work. Accessed via a narrow processional path resembling an ancient dromos, the main part of the memorial consists of two symmetrical concrete walls clad in stone forming a tight gateway that opens into a wider enclosure behind. A wrought-iron menorah stands at the far end of this space. Built into the walls are architectural fragments collected from the wartime ruins of Dorćol, Belgrade's traditionally Jewish neighborhood.

The memorial's meanings are complex and layered. Bogdanović claimed that he studied Kabbalah while working on the design, and some references to Jewish mysticism are indeed recognizable in the form. The two rounded walls resemble the Tablets of Stone on which Moses received the Ten Commandments,[7] whereas the sudden expansion of space after the tight compression between the walls may evoke Psalm 118:5: "I called upon the Lord in distress; The Lord answered me, and set me in a large place."[8] Later in his career, however, Bogdanović suggested other meanings, identifying the twin walls as "the wings of Ariel,"[9] "the sacred bird," and "the epiphany in the form of a bird," all of which are fundamentally different from (although not entirely incompatible with) more literal religious references.[10] Such deliberate injection of polysemy opened up the structure to the process of hermeneutics, casting the monument as something akin to a religious text, the meaning of which is never immediately transparent but requires active mental engagement.

The commission for the Jewish Victims monument opened an entirely new world for Bogdanović: commemorative architecture. It was also the basis for his future design method, in which the potentials of polysemy would continue to play a prominent role, albeit removed from a specific religious context. The meanings of his subsequent memorials thus became even more open-ended, stimulating free association and alluding to archetypal forms shared across great expanses of space and time. However, in contrast to religious hermeneutics, which ultimately seeks some form of spiritual revelation, for Bogdanović

FIG. 2. TWO VIEWS OF THE MONUMENT TO THE JEWISH VICTIMS OF FASCISM, BELGRADE, SERBIA. 1951-52

FIG. 3. THE MEMORIAL CEMETERY OF MURDERED PATRIOTS, BELGRADE, SERBIA. 1958-59

the process of interpretation became a goal in itself, ultimately serving as a vehicle for what Walter Benjamin called "profane illumination"— the desire to reenchant the world, albeit in distinctly secular terms, which lay at the core of the Surrealist project.[11] Indeed, always allusive but never literal, Bogdanović's memorials often blend competing references into ambiguous amalgams, not unlike the shapeshifting forms of Surrealist art that strive, as Breton famously demanded, to reveal the "actual functioning of thought."[12] Such an approach was fundamentally at odds with prevailing commemorative modes of the postwar period, not only in Yugoslavia but also at large, as it neither sought the ideological explicitness of Socialist Realist monuments nor mobilized the power of abstraction.

Considering Bogdanović's Surrealist background, it should come as no surprise that his initial study of Jewish mysticism would lead him toward mythology, anthropology, and ancient urban history: Surrealists cultivated a fascination with "primitive cultures" and the occult, seeking to recover the miraculous that had been expunged from modern civilization. The forms and arrangements of his memorials are thus reminiscent of all kinds of ancient motifs: tumuli, menhirs, stelae, petroglyphs, fortification walls, and symbolic gateways, as well as vernacular forms such as *stećci* (massive medieval tombstones) and *krajputaši* (simple roadside monuments, often dedicated to soldiers killed far away from home), both of which are found in large numbers around the former Yugoslavia.

Through careful manipulation of topography and vegetation, these different objects appear as if located in entirely pastoral settings, even when their actual sites were anything but pastoral. As a consequence, the memory of war casualties is displaced into an extremely *longue durée* perspective, tied into the cycles of natural changes, as a way of soothing the trauma of tragic violent deaths. *Nature and the Goddess of Remembrance*, the title of Bogdanović's award-winning exhibition representing Yugoslavia at the 1973 São Paulo Bienal, made such motivations explicit; the same is true of his photographs, in which nature often occupies the foreground and the built structure recedes into greenery.[13] But the goal of such framing (whether physical or photographic) was never to reify the transhistorical links or to fix a purported "natural essence" of commemoration; on the contrary, it was always to open up meaning as something flexible and fundamentally alive.

Despite the formative role of the Monument to the Jewish Victims of Fascism, it took several years after its completion for a new commemorative commission to materialize. The Memorial Cemetery of Murdered Patriots (1958–59) (fig. 3) at Belgrade's New Cemetery, which Bogdanović designed in collaboration with his former student Svetislav Ličina, contained an eclectic mix of elements and motifs, uncharacteristic of his subsequent, succinct work: an ornamental concrete enclosure with pyramidal mounds inside, a highly stylized freestanding Ionic colonnade, and even a scaled-down model

of the lampposts on which the victims of Nazi terror were hanged in downtown Belgrade during the war. It is perhaps due to such eclectic literalism that this work is rarely mentioned in the discussions of Bogdanović's oeuvre. The real breakthrough, however, came the following year, with the Memorial Cemetery for the Victims of Fascism (1959–60), in Sremska Mitrovica, Serbia (fig. 4). Located at the site of mass executions at the hands of Nazi and Ustaša (Croatian fascist) forces, the cemetery is dedicated to some eight thousand victims—predominantly civilians, but also Yugoslav Partisans and Red Army soldiers—murdered between 1941 and 1944. The large, landscaped complex is organized along a processional path that ends with the first of Bogdanović's proto-land-art interventions: eight earthen mounds of varied sizes, surrounding an irregularly shaped sunken paved area in the middle. Not only are there no ideological insignia here, there are almost no representational forms at all, save for the small flame-shaped bronze sculptures atop each mound. Despite its material modesty and formal restraint, the complex was well received, not only in Yugoslavia, but also abroad: it was featured in the French journal *L'architecture d'aujourd'hui*,[14] and the Italian architectural historian and theorist Bruno Zevi recommended it as a model for the memorial to the recently assassinated U.S. president John F. Kennedy.[15]

The complex in Sremska Mitrovica opened the door for the central commissions of Bogdanović's career, all of which originated at the turn of the 1960s. The twentieth anniversary of the 1941 uprising against fascist occupation brought a flurry of activities commemorating the war. The tenth anniversary had been marked rather modestly amid the crisis caused by Yugoslavia's surprising expulsion from the Soviet Bloc in 1948; a decade later, the country enjoyed the fruits of the reforms initiated in reaction to the events of 1948, most notably unprecedented economic growth and cultural liberalization, both of which began to attract international attention.[16] Under such conditions even the past war, with its endless trials and horrible suffering, could be cast in an optimistic light, as the origin of an ongoing prosperity. Monuments to different events of World War II, as well as to different categories of victims, all came to be subsumed under the common cause of commemorating the socialist revolution. Civilian casualties, Partisan fighters, Communist leaders, mass atrocities, acts of individual defiance, military battles, and the overall victory over fascism: in the emerging commemorative culture, everything began to coalesce into an indivisible whole that formed the foundation of socialist Yugoslavia. The need to give shape to this composite at the turn of the 1960s produced an extraordinary outburst of creativity that thoroughly reinvented the field of commemoration. Artists and architects such as Vojin Bakić, Zdenko Kolacio, Dušan Džamonja, and Miodrag Živković designed some of their most iconic works around this time, each developing a distinct personal poetic style based on varied degrees of abstraction. In many instances, their works projected a sense of defiance, if not outright triumphalism, as they sought to capture the spirit of a heroic victory achieved against all odds.

Four of Bogdanović's best-known projects, often described as his "tetralogy," originated around the same time. The memorial complexes in Mostar, Jasenovac, Prilep, and Kruševac were all important and widely praised contributions to the new culture of commemoration, but they project a more subdued, introspective atmosphere than other monuments built at the time. The shift in accent from the common themes of heroism and defiance to mourning is especially pronounced in the case of Jasenovac Memorial Site (1959–66) in Croatia and Slobodište Memorial Park (1960–65) in Kruševac, Serbia, which were built on the sites of mass atrocities. Both evoke funerary references—the flower on a gravesite in Jasenovac, Orphic iconography in Kruševac, and burial mounds in both instances—thus endowing the space with a vaguely sacred dimension unrelated to any specific religion.

This is not to say that these memorials wallow in misery and pessimism. On the contrary, throughout his career Bogdanović was adamant about the underlying message of all his work: "life overcomes death."[17] In addition to the diverse symbolism that his memorials invoke—for example, the hopeful flower sprouting from the blood-soaked soil in Jasenovac—they also convey this mantra in a more immediate way. Conceived as public parks, these monuments are meant to be sites of everyday life that bring the living and the dead into communion, rather than keep the two realms apart. This intended

use is made explicit by the amphitheatrical organization of the memorials in Kruševac, Vlasotince, and Leskovac, which allows them to be used for public performances.

In contrast to the defiant abstract sculptures of other Yugoslav artists that often produce their powerful effects through stark contrast with their surroundings, Bogdanović's memorials, as a rule, blend into the landscape or, more precisely, they *become* the landscape itself. This was especially characteristic of his key projects, which expanded on the extensive earthworks already established in Sremska Mitrovica. Combined with their deliberate archaism, these memorials inevitably bring to mind what in the late 1960s would become known as land art. The earthen craters of Slobodište certainly fall within this category; rising gently out of an unremarkable suburban environment, they set off a commemorative space that reads ambiguously as both natural and artificial. Earthworks are even more extensive in Mostar, where an entire cemetery is carved into the mountainside; however, in this case, the man-made character of the intervention is emphasized through massive retaining walls in stone, as well as an abundance of ornament.

The landscape holds by far the most symbolic role at Jasenovac Memorial Site, the location of a wartime concentration camp and mass murder. Here, Bogdanović originally planned what would have been his most extensive environmental intervention: to transform the entire area into a disorienting "primeval

13

waterscape," in which the land and the water from the nearby river Sava would come together to evoke the treacherous meanders, bends, and distributaries that prevented the prisoners from escaping the camp. However, anxious about disturbing the delicate balance of the waterways, Bogdanović eventually abandoned this idea and only retained two small ponds as a reminder that water, as much as land, was the victims' grave. It is no coincidence that the central flower-shaped marker rises out of one of these ponds. Even the greatly downscaled earthworks are symbolic: the circular mounds scattered throughout the park mark the locations of the concentration camp buildings, which had been destroyed in the early postwar years, thus producing what could be termed a topography of suffering.

Bogdanović's later memorials did not match the ambitions of those from the 1960s, but careful siting remained a distinct feature of his work. The majority of his memorials are located on the outskirts of cities and towns, often because that was where mass killings occurred during the war. In such cases, Bogdanović sought to establish a sensitive relationship between the commemorative site and the city, one that allowed the dead to rest in peace undisturbed by the bustle of daily life, but did not isolate them from the community or allow their sacrifice to dominate the living. This strategy is especially obvious in Bogdanović's use of elevated landscapes. The only monument that occupies the peak of a hill and is immediately noticeable from the city below is the Shrine to the Fallen Serb

and Albanian Partisans (1960–73) in Mitrovica/Mitrovicë, Kosovo. In all other cases—in Mostar, Leskovac, Vlasotince, Štip, and Čačak—the memorials are tucked into the slope, remaining almost imperceptible from below, though they offer striking views of the city in situ.[18] The Partisan Memorial Cemetery (1959–65) in Mostar, Bosnia and Herzegovina, explicitly conceived as a "city of the dead" facing the city of the living below, complete with its own protective walls and streets, is an especially apt example of this approach.

In addition to the approach to siting, several other themes are consistent throughout Bogdanović's entire career, though always articulated in a different way and with a fundamentally different meaning. For example, the concept of the memorial as a cluster of objects can be traced back to the Mound of the Undefeated (Partisan Necropolis), the project for Prilep, Macedonia, in the early 1960s, and we see it appear repeatedly over the following two decades, up until one of Bogdanović's last works, Dudik Memorial Park (1978–80) in Vukovar, Croatia. However, the shape that these objects take, as well as the way in which they are organized, varies greatly: most of the time, the ornamental stelae, cones, quasi-anthropomorphic figures, or just pieces of rock lie in loose, seemingly random configurations, but in a few cases they form irregular closed ovals (as in the Freedom Monument at Jasikovac [1972–77] in Berane, Montenegro, and the Memorial to Fallen Freedom Fighters [1973–75] in Vlasotince, Serbia). The same can be said of Bogdanović's reliance on ornament: while most of the memorials are highly decorative (a deliberate slap in the face to modernist orthodoxy), they differ in both their language and their material execution: from crude petroglyphs to delicate, precise carvings to complex composites of stone blocks. And just to make things even more complicated, in the cases of Jasenovac and Popina Memorial Park (1978–81), near Trstenik, Serbia, the form may be highly symbolic, but there is no conventional ornament at all.

There is a certain degree of self-reference in Bogdanović's oeuvre that lends it a deceptive sense of consistency, repeatedly undermined by startling exceptions in his most important works. Most of his projects were built using archaic stoneworking techniques, but his most iconic and widely known creation, the flower at the Jasenovac Memorial Site, is a tour de force of modern engineering in reinforced concrete. Many of his projects were celebrations of organicism that allowed a degree of free interpretation in their execution, but the first and the last major piece, the Monument to the Jewish Victims and Popina Memorial Park, are both exercises in geometric precision and careful proportioning. As a consequence, it would be virtually impossible to construct an ideal prototype of a Bogdanović memorial or to clearly establish his "style," even though his own photos tend to offer a strongly idiosyncratic perspective that always empha-sizes the communion between his built work and nature. What he created, rather, was a method of design that dug deep into the human mind

and collective memory as a way of stimulating free, unbound, creative thought. The result was a world unto its own, a world that is simultaneously comforting and bewildering, materially tangible and surreal. This book offers a glimpse into that world through the eyes of its creator.

•••

I first met Bogdan Bogdanović as an undergraduate student at the University of Belgrade's Faculty of Architecture some time in the early 1990s. I visited him with a group of friends, all architecture students; we were the first generation since the early 1950s whom he did not teach, having retired just before we enrolled. His spirit, however, still loomed in the guise of his many former students who had ascended to teaching positions. By the time of our visit, the war that would tear Yugoslavia apart was already raging. Bogdan and his wife, Ksenija, greeted us in their darkened apartment in downtown Belgrade, window shutters closed and curtains pulled so that no signs of life would be visible from the outside. Once one of Yugoslavia's most prominent architects and the former mayor of Belgrade, Bogdanović was now a pariah because he dared raise his voice against ascending nationalism to become one of the earliest and most vocal opponents of Milošević's regime. State media waged a bitter campaign against him. Climbing up to the apartment, we could see threats scribbled on the walls of the stairwell. Despite the conspiratorial atmo-sphere—or perhaps precisely because of it—the conversation was mesmerizing; Bogdanović was a charismatic speaker and it did not take much to enchant a group of young students already primed to receive his message. There was something simultaneously surreal and soothing about sitting in that cavernous residence filled with books, discussing ancient symbology—as if we were clinging to the last shred of optimism while outside the world as we knew it was falling apart.

Not long after our visit, Bogdan and Ksenija left Belgrade, eventually finding refuge in Vienna. Neither would ever return to their native city, save for a few short visits. More than a decade would pass before I saw them again. This time, it was in 2004 in Vienna, where I came to study German as a graduate student. A decade of war and destruction was behind us, but some of the memorials did not survive it unscathed. Encouraged by our renewed encounter, I returned the following year to interview Bogdanović as part of my dissertation research. Ksenija was in Belgrade at the time, packing up the architect's archive to be transferred to the Architekturzentrum Wien, in Vienna, so he welcomed the company. I ended up staying an entire week. We had a glorious time together: we talked every day for seven or eight hours about all kinds of topics, from politics and his experiences as mayor of Belgrade to his wartime memories and his memorials. We would end each day with a glass of wine or liquor, which was when some of the best conversations occurred—with my recording device switched off. It was then that I first saw the images that ultimately inspired this book, projected on the Bogdanovićs' dining room wall via a massive metal contraption that was already obsolete. Bogdan commented on the slides as I listened, recording his words and asking an occasional question.

After Bogdan's death in 2010, I stayed in touch with Ksenija, and I visited her whenever I was in Europe. During one of these visits, in 2013 or 2014, we came to the conclusion that it would be worth trying to publish the photos that I had seen almost a decade earlier. The stars aligned in favor of the idea: my friend Wolfgang Thaler quickly arranged for us to use the scanning equipment of his colleagues in the artists' collective Gelitin; another friend, Jelica Jovanović, was willing to dedicate several weeks to digitizing around 150 slides in high resolution, and a Graham Foundation grant that I had just received to research Bogdanović's oeuvre covered some of the cost. Not long after, The Museum of Modern Art announced its interest in organizing an exhibition about the architecture of socialist Yugoslavia, with Bogdanović's work as one of the highlights. The book started to seem possible. Ksenija was very excited about the prospect; we shared our enthusiasm once again in early September 2017 when I stopped by to see her in Vienna on one of my transatlantic trips. She walked around her apartment hooked up to an oxygen tank, but I was sure I would be able to show her the final product. Less than two weeks later, she passed away. I am sad that she never got to see this book. The coincidence that I am completing the manuscript on her ninety-third birthday is only a minor consolation.

What follows are excerpts from the conversations I had with Bogdanović during that splendid week in May 2005, accompanied by a selection of the slides that he showed me. Not all of his works are included here—only the ones he chose to share with me on that occasion. A much larger set of photographs is stored at the Architekturzentrum Wien, together with a vast collection of Bogdanović's masterful drawings. If this book inspires anyone to dive into that treasure, my mission will be complete.

Princeton, December 25, 2017

Notes

1. For Belgrade Surrealists, see Sanja Bahun-Radunović, "When the Margin Cries: Surrealism in Yugoslavia," *RiLUnE*, no. 3 (2005): 37-52; and "Surréalistes Serbes," ed. Henri Béhar and Jelena Novaković, special issue of *Mélusine*, no. XXX (2010).

2. The Yugoslav controversy became known as the "conflict on the literary left," which placed Ristić and Krleža's calls for creative freedom in opposition to the party leaders' push for explicit political tendentiousness.

3. For Bogdanović's writings on the city, see Vladimir Vuković, *Bogdan Bogdanović: Das literarische Werk* (Vienna: Anton Pustet Verlag, 2009). See also Vladimir Kulić, "Bogdan Bogdanović and the Search for a Meaningful City," in *East West Central: Re-Building Europe, 1950-1990*, Volume 1, edited by Ákos Moravánskzky, Torsten Lange, Judith Hopfengärtner, and Karl R. Kegler (Basel: Birkhäuser Verlag, 2016), 77-88.

4. Bogdan Bogdanović, *Zaludna mistrija. Doktrina i praktika zlatnih (crnih) brojeva* (Belgrade: Nolit, 1963).

5. For Bogdanović's relationship to postmodernism, see Vladimir Kulić, "Bogdan Bogdanović's Surrealist Postmodernism," in the forthcoming book *Second World Postmodernisms: Architecture and Society under Late Socialism*, ed. Kulić (London: Bloomsbury, 2018).

6. Aurel Spiler, "Spomenik jevrejskim žrtvama fašističkog terora na Jevrejskom groblju u Beogradu" (A monument to Jewish victims of fascist terror at the Jewish Cemetery in Belgrade), Architekturzentrum Wien, Vienna, NO5-002-001-Dok / 1-1.

7. I am grateful to David Raizman for the reference. It had been already identified by Bogdanović's contemporaries; see Katarina Ambrozić, "Bogdan Bogdanović: The Artist and His Work," in *Nature and the Goddess of Remembrance*, exh. cat. (Belgrade: Museum of Modern Art, 1973), n.p.

8. I thank Moishe Postone for suggesting the reference to this Psalm.

9. Ariel is an angel from Jewish and Christian mysticism, often depicted with a lion's head. Ariel is sometimes conflated with another deity from the Judeo-Christian tradition, Archangel Uriel, the guardian of the gate of Eden.

10. *Nature and the Goddess of Remembrance*, n.p.

11. Walter Benjamin, "Surrealism: The Last Snapshot of the European Intelligentsia," in *Walter Benjamin: Selected Writings, Vol. 2, 1927-1934*, ed. Michael W. Jennings, Howard Eiland, and Gary Smith (Cambridge, Mass.: Harvard University Press, 1999), 207-21.

12. André Breton, *Manifestoes of Surrealism*, trans. Richard Seaver and Helen R. Lane (Ann Arbor: University of Michigan Press, 1969), 26.

13. *Nature and the Goddess of Remembrance*.

14. D[anielle] Valeix, "Cimetière commémoratif, Sremska Mitrovica," *L'architecture d'aujourd'hui*, no. 108 (1963): 74-75.

15. Bruno Zevi, "Cimiteri che parlano da Sremska Mitrovica" (The Speaking Cemeteries of Sremska Mitrovica), *L'Espresso*, December 15, 1963.

16. Nineteen sixty-one was indeed a remarkable year for Yugoslavia's global reputation: Ivo Andrić won the Nobel Prize in Literature, Dušan Vukotić was the first foreigner to win an Oscar for an animated short, and in September, Belgrade hosted the founding summit of the Non-Aligned Movement, which inaugurated the country's role as an important player in international politics.

17. *Nature and the Goddess of Remembrance*.

18. The memorials in Bihać and Novi Travnik sit atop small hillocks, but both are too far from their respective towns to dominate them. The memorial in Berane is surrounded by a thick forest and is virtually invisible until one gets close to it. Popina Memorial Park is completely outside any urban area and can only be glimpsed from the road below.

Bogdanović in Conversation

with Vladimir Kulić

Over the course of five days in late May 2005, I recorded a series of conversations I had with Bogdan Bogdanović, who was then retired and living in exile in Vienna. The following excerpts capture the spirit and substance of our wide-ranging discussion.

When you look back on your career, what gives you the greatest satisfaction?

The diversity of my pursuits. I was an architect, an urbanist, a writer, even a politician. I could have chosen to be just one of these things and I probably would have ended up being a *fachidiot*. Instead, the variety of my interests allowed me to understand the world from multiple perspectives, as if it were reflected in multiple mirrors. But I always remained an architect in spirit. I enjoyed how I was able to organize my own work, to collaborate directly with craftsmen on the construction site, often improvising. With the exception of Jasenovac [Memorial Site in Croatia], everything I built could have been done in the third millennium before Christ. Such archaism was my deliberate choice.

In addition to wearing these different hats, you were also a public intellectual. How would you describe your intellectual origins?

As early as high school, I began to consider myself a Surrealist. That was the result of family circumstances. I met [Serbian Surrealist writer] Marko Ristić as a teenager, and he impressed me greatly; he was a first-class intellectual and an exceptional figure. Only many years later did I realize that he was [Jorge Luis] Borges's doppelgänger. He was half blind like Borges, but they also physically resembled one another. Ristić was a great teacher of mine. As a result, I was quickly disenchanted with modernism—or modernisms—especially those with pro-Fascist inclinations, like Italian Futurism. The Surrealists did not consider themselves modernists; the latter were ideologically all over the place. In contrast, Surrealism was a consistent, complete philosophy—perhaps because it was so complete it could not develop much further after the war. But Surrealism was the foundation to which I always returned. Even back then, as a high school student, I believed that my mission in life was to make an *architecture surrealiste.* But that ambition was problematic; it was very much at odds with the prevailing mood, which favored the rational, strict, hard Corbusian approach. In such a climate, it was very difficult to make architecture out of the quiet, subterranean poetry of dreams and the unconscious.

Belgrade Surrealists were also strongly politicized.

Yes. When I enrolled in architecture, just before the outbreak of the Second World War, I was already leftist in orientation. At that time, there was a great confrontation on the left: Ristić and [Miroslav] Krleža opposed Socialist Realism, which was the official line of the Communist Party. Later on, in Tito's postwar Yugoslavia, I was accused of being a Trotskyist because of my links with the Surrealists. Trotskyism was a common accusation: everyone who was firmly leftist, but not willing to submit to the pro-Soviet hard line, was considered a Trotskyist.

I never thought I would build monuments. I thought of myself as a Surrealist and a leftist, but I still assumed that I would build pretty villas. My ideal was Adolf Loos's Tristan Tzara House [1926] in Paris. That was something I would have enjoyed making. During those dark wartime years, Ristić titillated my imagination by asking me to design a house for him. Perhaps it wasn't an entirely hypothetical project, because he was from a wealthy bourgeois family and he may have been expecting an inheritance from someone. But life writes its own stories: when the war ended, Ristić became the ambassador of Communist Yugoslavia in Paris, and I returned from the Partisans to continue my architecture studies.

Tell me about your time with the People's Liberation Movement.

I joined the Partisans rather late, in the summer of 1944, but I took my short participation in the war very seriously. I not only joined the Communist Party, but I also became a deputy commissar of the battalion. I was badly wounded in the hip on February 1, 1945, and only left the hospital two months after the war ended. For a while, I was in rough shape not only physically, but also psychologically; I had periodic inflammations of the wound and additional surgeries, not to mention the pain. I think I was admitted to the hospital six more times. The morphine they gave me was great: the pain was still there, but it was no longer mine. And my fantasy went into overdrive. Every noise from the outside world sounded like a piano concerto, even if it were a teaspoon dropped next door. I think I told the doctors I liked morphine, so they took me off it. "He's dangerous, no more morphine for him." So I had to suffer again.

Finally, you went back to studying architecture.

Yes. The Falculty of Architecture in Belgrade reopened in the late fall of 1945, but I fell behind my cohort because of my heavy political engagement. I also underwent a personal crisis related to my future professional life. I was an excellent student with high grades, but I couldn't imagine doing what everyone else was doing at the time. In those first postwar years, architectural design was almost as if under military control. There were great material shortages and there were special committees to prevent any kind of excess or inefficiency. It was truly depressing. I realized that I would be useless as an architect under such conditions, so I decided that it was best to turn to urban planning. At least there was some scientific knowledge involved in it, and the course of study enabled one to think about the city beyond what the practice demanded.

When did you graduate?

I graduated in 1950, having completed my thesis under Nikola Dobrović on the urban regulation of the island of Lapad near Dubrovnik.[1] I was then hired as an assistant in the Department of Urban Planning in the Faculty of Architecture.

However, shortly thereafter you built the Monument to the Jewish Victims of Fascism in Belgrade. How did that happen?

The Jewish memorial [1951–52] was my turning point. That project opened an entirely new world for me. To begin work on it, I had to learn about symbols and metaphors. I studied Kabbalah and Jewish esotericism, and I suddenly realized that it was all a part of the broader world of esotericism linked to antiquity. That's when I established my relationship to tradition. It didn't come through vernacular architecture, or through our medieval monasteries, but through ancient mysticism.

What is it that came from Kabbalah in that project?

Transcendence. It marks the transition from one sphere to another. It is not just in Kabbalah; most esoteric traditions contain the same idea. Rituals often concern gateways, even in

Christianity, and especially in Orthodoxy. There were no trees behind the monument at the time it was built, so it framed a view of the sky. At the opening, one of the guests, a French Jewish woman, exclaimed, "Mon Dieu, c'est une vue vers l'éternité!" I was ecstatic! And then I expected everyone to realize that I was a master. But nothing happened. I was convinced that I'd made something good, but my colleagues weren't terribly impressed.

Why not? Was it incomprehensible?
I think so. Truth be told, it was probably the first abstract memorial in Yugoslavia. Had I made a realistic sculpture—for example, something showing the victims of an execution—it would have been fine. But this was something different. To make it worse, the devil then pushed me to start writing. I wrote about the city very differently from how urbanism was conceived at the time. It was provocative. Writing was both my curse and my most powerful weapon.

It had considerable impact, didn't it?
Do you know what made an impact? The book *Small Urbanism* (1958). In it, I mocked the "big urbanism," its deadly seriousness. People were quick to understand that urbanism was not what urban planners were telling them, but what they saw with their own eyes. And what did they see? They saw sparrows and pigeons, they saw people in the streets, they saw the deserted city at night. Today it is completely normal to speak about the city in those terms—if what we have today can be considered cities at all. But back then, it was a time of grand ideas and grand gestures. In New Belgrade they were constructing buildings six hundred meters long. I thought it was a catastrophe.

So, what were the alternatives? What were the models to which you could subscribe?
I deeply respect Jože Plečnik, perhaps I even adore him. I was initiated into Plečnik's world as a freshman in college. I found his book *Architectura Perennis* [1941] in a used bookstore,

I think during the occupation. Plečnik's world is still more relevant than much of what came after him; it's a universe of its own. I also discovered [Karl Friedrich] Schinkel during the occupation; I got his monograph from a street vendor, some local Gavroche who must have stolen it from a building destroyed in the bombing. I immediately spotted the Schinkel, but I pretended to be interested in something else to get the price down.

Why Schinkel?
I was really impressed with his drawings. They spoke to me very clearly. It still delights me how he played with architectural history. I loved his architectural fantasies, for example, how he moved the Strasbourg cathedral around, how he displaced it to some distant Germanic forests, or how he moved the Milan cathedral to the Mediterranean coast, into olive groves. That kind of thinking attracted me greatly. I suddenly understood the joy of architecture. During the war, I also discovered [Claude-Nicolas] Ledoux at the library of the Technical Faculty. I think I must have seen a Surrealist thread in him.

I have to admit that, at the time, I saw all these fascinations as a guilty pleasure. Le Corbusier was Le Corbusier, after all, and I thought that I'd be something like him. But in hiding even from myself, I found Schinkel much more interesting. In a way, Ristić must have pushed me in that direction. Surrealists didn't care for Le Corbusier.

What attracted you to Surrealism in the first place?
It opened an entire world for me. I was a bit of a pretentious kid. The first Surrealist that I truly understood and embraced was Man Ray. He was not yet well known at the time. When I first saw his rayographs, my father explained to me how they were made and later on I tried to improvise making some. I cut a few figures out of paper and pinned them to a curtain in the vestibule, and I glued a couple on a glass door, and I waited for the reflecting light to take the picture. When my father saw these photos, he

was delighted because he thought they were real rayographs, but he could not figure out how I had made them. When I explained, he got really mad; in his view, they were completely fake. My technique wasn't *lege artis*.

But what you did was quite inventive.
Well, yes. You see, it seems that I was destined for Surrealism.

You told me earlier that you started photographing even before you were able to read.
I took my first photo just before I started the first grade. I couldn't yet read or write. That fall I got a Box-Tengor camera; it was a children's camera, made for beginners. In my delight, I immediately tried to take a photo of my sister, but she got scared and turned her back to me. So I took the picture from the back. Everyone wondered why I decided to photograph my sister that way. Later on, at our family estate in eastern Serbia, I took several series of photos of people from the back, because the villagers would always stiffen up in front of the camera; from the back, I could catch them behaving spontaneously.

Both my grandfather and my father were photographers. My grandfather used to drag around some massive camera on a tripod, and my father worked with plate cameras, and later on he had a Leica.

What kind of camera did you use to shoot the monuments?
Around the time of the Belgrade Conference in 1961, I received a big honorarium, which rarely happened to me.[2] It must have been as much as two or three months of my university salary. On such occasions, I always spent the money on books. However, at this time the stores were stocked with foreign goods because many foreign guests were expected to come to town for the conference. In one of the shop windows downtown, I spotted a Japanese Mamiyaflex camera. That was the first time I saw a dual lens camera. For a long time, that was the pinnacle of technology. So there I am, with the honorarium in my pocket, all unkempt, because at the time I didn't care much about dressing up. I walked in and I said bluntly, "I want to buy the Mamiyaflex." The salesman looked at me suspiciously and asked, "Wouldn't you like to take a look at it first?" And I just said, "No, I'll take it." After I paid, I saw him going behind a partition to check in front of a lamp to see if the money was forged. That's how I became the owner of a Mamiyaflex. Everything I'm going to show you was shot with it. Later on, I looked for a smaller format, because this was a heavy camera. But I could never take such marvelous photos as with the Mamiyaflex.

Vienna, May 21–25, 2005

Our final conversation ended with a slideshow in Bogdanović's dining room, in which he projected photographs he'd taken of a number of his monuments and told anecdotes about their making. These striking images and excerpts from his commentary, as well as some of my additional editorial notes, appear on the following pages.

Notes
1. Nikola Dobrović (1897–1967) was an influential Serbian and Yugoslav modernist architect and writer who joined the Faculty of Architecture in Belgrade in 1948 and taught there until his death. Dobrović's key works include several modernist villas built in Dubrovnik in the 1930s, and the monumental Generalštab building (Federal Secretariat of Defense and the Headquarters of the Yugoslav People's Army, 1954–63) in Belgrade.
2. The first Conference of Heads of State or Government of Non-Aligned Countries, held in Belgrade in early September 1961. The conference was the effective inauguration of the Non-Aligned Movement.

Mound of the Undefeated (Partisan Necropolis)
Prilep, Macedonia. 1960–61

Commissioned by the local municipality, this site commemorates the eight hundred local Partisan fighters killed in World War II. It consists of a commemorative mound and a plateau in front of it featuring a group of eight stone figures. The mound has an open-air cavity at its center, which can be entered from the plateau to access the names of the deceased carved into marble walls. Today, the memorial is well maintained as part of a larger public park.

The arrangement suggests figures dancing. We produced two more foundations than the actual number of figures in order to have a bit of leeway in finding the best configuration. Some future archaeologist will theorize why there were extra foundations. I designed the largest of the figures by drawing it on the wall of my studio from different angles. So the figure ended up being as tall as the ceiling height would allow. —BOGDAN BOGDANOVIĆ

Everything finds its place.
Everything has already been invented.

Partisan Memorial Cemetery
Mostar, Bosnia and Herzegovina. 1959–65

One of Bogdanović's most extensive projects, the cemetery honors
Partisans from the region around the city of Mostar killed in World War II.
Names of some eight hundred known fighters are carved into
gravestones laid out on several terraces; an additional several hundred
unidentified bodies rest in a collective tomb. After being restored
in the mid-2000s, the cemetery suffered renewed vandalism and neglect.
As of April 2018, another restoration of the complex was underway.

This was a monument to Yugoslav solidarity.
It was dedicated to the Mostar battalion.
What was most touching to me was that the
soldiers were practically children. Their names:
Muslim, Serbian, Croatian. It reminded me
of the Children's Crusades. A huge percentage
were killed. These are cenotaphs, symbolic
graves. Some remains were buried here, but
not very many.

The memorial is badly defaced, but it couldn't be demolished—it is carved into the hill, so it's indestructible

Slobodište Memorial Park
Kruševac, Serbia. 1960-65

This park commemorates the site where the German army executed
more than sixteen hundred local civilians and resistance fighters between
1941 and 1944. The larger of the two earthen amphitheaters Bogdanović
designed for the memorial is used for performances, whereas the smaller one,
containing twelve stone sculptures, serves a purely symbolic function.
The site is still in active use and is well cared for.

I asked a group of schoolchildren to help me organize the figures. I would give them wooden sticks to use as markers and then I'd let them play around. I'd tell them, "Stand there," and they would mark the spots with the sticks. Then I would move them around to try a new configuration. They were very excited. I saw it as a link between architecture and choreography.

Jasenovac Memorial Site
Jasenovac, Croatia. 1959–66

Jasenovac was the largest wartime concentration camp in Yugoslavia,
run between 1941 and 1945 by the Ustaša regime of the quisling
Independent State of Croatia. More than eighty thousand victims—mostly Serbs,
Jews, and Roma, but also ethnic Croat dissenters—have been identified,
but it is estimated that at least one hundred thousand people died here. The park
was commissioned by the Union of the Liberation War Veterans Associations
of Yugoslavia and remains a major site of memory. In 2007, it was awarded
the International Carlo Scarpa Prize for Gardens.

In all my projects, and especially at Jasenovac, the idea never developed in a linear fashion. I always ran in circles. In this case, I designed an entire world of flowers. At first, there were many; later I condensed them all into one. I analyzed different flowers, their types, their interior mechanics. Today that would have been easier to do with a computer, but perhaps the computer would make it too easy.

As you go around the flower, you experience three alternating elevations. There is a mathematical formula to the shape. A sculptor would have made it differently: sculptors work with their hands, whereas here everything was drawn, calculated, geometrically resolved. When people ask what the difference is between an architectural and a sculptural memorial, my answer is that an architectural memorial can be described mathematically. Everything you see is a part of a cone or a sphere.

Nevertheless, it is a very complex shape, so the formwork was a huge problem. An old engineer advised me to invite traditional shipbuilders from Dalmatia for the job. That was crucial.

Monument to the Revolution
Leskovac, Serbia. 1964–71

This memorial—composed of a central forty-foot-tall figure and approximately three dozen stelae of varying heights—is a cenotaph for the liberation fighters and civilians from Leskovac and its vicinity killed in World War II. Some of the stelae bear the names of local heroes of the resistance movement. The monument is an active site of commemoration; although not entirely neglected, the pavement is damaged, several stelae have been overturned, and the central figure lacks the ornamental pendants that originally hung from its crown.

This is a theatrical form or, should I say, choreographic.
There was always a bit of ballet involved in my projects.
The local Roma kids nicknamed the central figure—
guess what? Elizabeth Taylor! I found that very
encouraging, because it showed me that the feminine
form that I intended to build really came through.

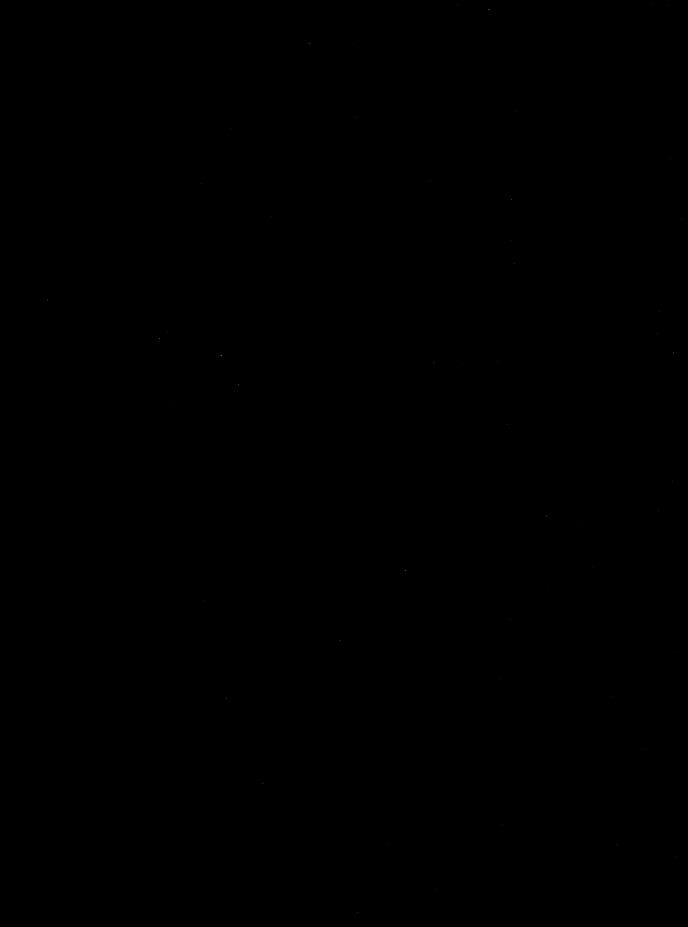

Memorial Park to the Fallen Fighters
in the Liberation Wars 1804–1945
Knjaževac, Serbia. 1969–71

The park was designed to commemorate local victims of all the region's
liberation wars, from the First Serbian Uprising against the Turkish
occupation of 1804 to that fought by the Partisans during World War II.
Situated in the heart of the town, the memorial park remains well maintained

This memorial is in the heart of Knjaževac.
It's the history of the small town since the Turkish
wars, condensed in stone. These stelae are
derived from traditional beehives, which used to
be decorated with beautiful ornaments. There
is a bit of a Byzantine painting influence as well.

Shrine to the Fallen Serb and Albanian Partisans
Mitrovica/Mitrovicë, Kosovo. 1960–73

This monument is dedicated to the fallen ethnic Albanian and Serb Partisans,
members of a miners' platoon. They successfully sabotaged the extraction
of zinc and lead ore from the Trepča mines, which the occupying German forces
needed for weapons production. Most of the copper cladding
of the memorial's lintel is now missing.

This was one of my most complicated projects. It took some ten or twelve years from the first sketches to realization. The monument is dedicated to the Partisans. The two pylons were often interpreted as a Serb and an Albanian figure. In my interactions with the local clients, Serbs and Albanians seemed to work well together; later, I found it very painful when the trouble in Kosovo began.

I wanted to symbolize a gateway or entrance. The main generator for the form was space—the enormous open space with fantastic depth overlooking the city. I explored many different directions before I came up with this version, which stands its own ground against the vast empty space. As it turns out, it now sits precisely on the border between the Serb and Albanian parts of the city.

Adonis's Altar
Labin, Croatia. 1973–74

This noncommemorative sculpture was produced for a sculptors' colony.
A decade after its construction, Bogdanović used the altar's form
as the basis for the Guardian of Freedom, his monument to the fallen
resistance fighters in Klis, near Split. (Dating from 1982–87, the
Guardian of Freedom was destroyed just after the Croatian War of
Independence as part of a massive campaign for the
destruction of Yugoslav antifascist memorials.)

There was a sculptors' symposium in Labin, to which I was invited to contribute a piece. I was studying mythology at the time and I proposed to make an altar to Adonis. Adonis was beautiful, but I interpreted him ironically: this one is a bit clumsy, his head is too large, and his butt, too. Adonis was a deity governing the change of seasons, so the piece symbolizes one season on each of its four sides.

Necropolis for the Victims of Fascism
Novi Travnik, Bosnia and Herzegovina. 1971–75

Located atop a low hill between the towns of Travnik and Novi Travnik, this cenotaph, which comprises a dozen megaliths, commemorates the site of the Ustaša regime's mass execution in 1941 of seven hundred Serb civilians from the Travnik area. It suffered extensive damage from shelling and gunfire during the 1990s and remains in poor shape.

vrlik was my best and
. It is entirely Surreal in
 it to an archaeologist,
ean, that there is some-
luding the omega, the

e time I built it, so I didn't
 a story of mythical
ha is a two-headed serpent
 ection and by night in
 end of time.

Memorial to Fallen Freedom Fighters, 1941–45
Vlasotince, Serbia. 1973–75

This monument is dedicated to the fallen soldiers of
the antifascist resistance, as well as civilian victims of fascism.
Although routinely cared for today, it is defaced by graffiti.

This was a very modest memorial, built from the kind of stone that is usually only ground for gravel. It certainly wouldn't be used for proper stone carving. There is an amphitheater in the middle: a real oval amphitheater where one can perform, recite, dance, sit.

I made a large collection of ornamental drawings in stone. I had an assistant with me, a kid who helped me carry a bucket with watered-down ink, with which I made the drawings directly on the stone to be carved. If I made a mistake, there was another bucket with clear water to wash the drawing away. And I drew and drew. These will be my longest-lasting drawings.

Freedom Monument at Jasikovac
Berane, Montenegro. 1972–77

Built at the location where Italian occupying forces shot nine patriots
in July 1941, this monument commemorates the history of liberation
struggles in the region of Berane from the nineteenth century to World War II.
The site remains in good condition.

Here is the site of an old Turkish earthen fortification, on top of the hill overlooking the town. There is a small valley at the very top, from which one sees nothing but sky.

This is the area of Montenegro inhabited by the Vasojević clan. The clients wanted to show the entire history of the clan. We made a deal to carve their history into these granite blocks surrounding the cone.

Everything you see on the blocks are variations
on themes from women's costumes. These women
hide flames and heavenly beasts in their ornament.
So much suppressed passion goes into the ornament
on their costume. Even though it is women's clothing,
it's heroic. I'm very proud of this memorial.

Mausoleum of Struggle and Victory
Čačak, Serbia. 1970–80

This memorial is dedicated to the 4,650 fallen soldiers of the People's Liberation Movement killed between 1941 and 1945. It includes an ossuary containing the remains of several hundred local fighters and civilians. Today the site is a popular, well-kept public park, but the stone structures are covered in graffiti.

I originally calculated that I needed twelve monsters for the upper pylons. But the stone carvers liked working on these figures; as they carved, they would yell to each other: "Look, here's a boar!" "Here's a lion!" "Here's a pig!" And they started demanding, "Give us more, mister architect!" Why? Because we were finalizing the commission and soon they would be out of work. I could tell that the client had more money, so I started expanding the job to include more monsters. There are hundreds of beasts and no two are the same. The craftsmen ended up earning quite a handsome fee.

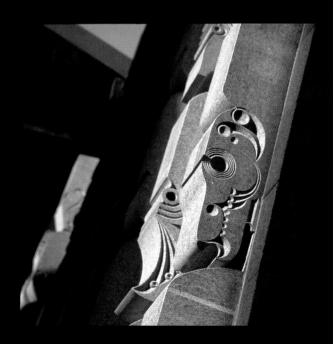

The metaphor here is a house under attack.
I'm not sure if I consciously anticipated what would
happen with Yugoslavia. But I think I had a fear.

Dudik Memorial Park
Vukovar, Croatia. 1978–80

This memorial stands on the grounds of mass executions
of civilians and resistance fighters conducted by the Ustaša
regime between 1941 and 1943. Badly damaged in the Serbian siege
of Vukovar during the Croatian War of Independence in the 1990s,
it was rebuilt in 2015, largely to its original form.

Vukovar is one of my last projects. This is how it looked originally. Now one of the caps is down, another one was damaged by shelling. I found two old craftsmen who specialized in repairing church bell towers. One of the metaphors was a cathedral buried underground, and the tops are indeed like local bell towers: there is a wooden structure underneath and copper cladding on the outside.

The small stelae are *chaikas* [river boats used in early modern Central and Eastern Europe]. They were once common in the area

Garavice Memorial Park

Bihać, Bosnia and Herzegovina. 1969–81

The park is dedicated to the Serb and Jewish civilians killed in 1941
by the Ustaša regime, as well as to the fallen resistance fighters
who liberated the region in 1942 to form the short-lived Bihać Republic.
The memorial was designated a National Monument of Bosnia and Herzegovina.
It remains partially damaged from the 1990s fighting.

Female metaphors dominate all my memorials, including this one. That's how it is in the history of commemoration; it is the female form that records. I didn't talk about that; I lived among epic, heroic people who cherished their masculinity. I knew that I wanted this form to read as a female figure, but I didn't want any literal references to the human shape. Some poet called these figures the "unmerry wives of Bihać." By the way, it was all built without any mortar; it's heavy block upon heavy block.

Popina Memorial Park
Popina near Trstenik, Serbia. 1978–81

Commissioned by the neighboring municipalities of Trstenik and Vrnjačka Banja, the park commemorates the Battle of Popina, fought between Partisan troops and the occupying German forces in October 1941. The memorial was recently restored and the site remains in good condition.

This was the site of one of the first battles against
the German occupation of Serbia in World War II.
Here you find yourself within a gun's sight. It's disturbing

What I'm most proud of is that my monuments
are linked to the memorials of all past times.
They form a brotherhood among themselves.

Bogdan Bogdanović: Selected Writings

(Cited by date of first edition)

Mali urbanizam (*Small Urbanism*). Sarajevo: Narodna prosvjeta, 1958.

Zaludna mistrija: Doktrina i praktika bratstva zlatnih (crnih) brojeva (*The Futile Trowel: The Doctrine and Practice of the Brotherhood of Golden [Black] Numbers*). Belgrade: Nolit, 1963.

Urbanističke mitologeme (*Urban Mythologems*). Belgrade: Vuk Karadžić, 1966.

Nature and the Goddess of Remembrance, exhibition catalogue. Belgrade: Museum of Modern Art, 1973.

"Town and Town Mythology." *Ekistics* 35, no. 209 (April 1973): 240–42.

"Symbols in the City and the City as a Symbol." *Ekistics* 39, no. 232 (March 1975): 140–46.

Urbs & logos: ogledi iz simbologije grada (*Urbs and logos: Essays on Urban Symbolism*). Niš, Serbia: Gradina, 1976.

Povratak grifona: crtačka heuristička igra po modelu Luisa Karola (*The Return of the Gryphon: A Drawing Heuristic Game Modeled on Lewis Carroll*). Vrnjačka Banja, Serbia: Zamak kulture, 1978.

Gradoslovar (*Urbolexicon*). Belgrade: Vuk Karadžić, 1982.

Krug na četiri ćoška (*The Four-Cornered Circle*). Belgrade: Nolit, 1986.

Mrtvouzice: mentalne zamke Staljinizma (*Dead Knots: The Mental Traps of Stalinism*). Zagreb: August Cesarec, 1988.

Knjiga kapitela (*The Book of Capitals*). Sarajevo: Svjetlost, 1990.

Die Stadt und der Tod (*The City and Death*). Klagenfurt, Austria: Wieser Verlag, 1993.

Die Stadt und die Zukunft: Essay (*The City and the Future: An Essay*). Klagenfurt, Austria: Wieser Verlag, 1997.

Der verdammte Baumeister: Erinnerungen (*The Accursed Master Builder: Memories*). Vienna: Paul Zsolnay Verlag, 1997.

Vom Glück in dem Städten (*On Happiness in Cities*). Vienna: Paul Zsolnay Verlag, 2002.

Die Grüne Schachtel: Buch der Träume (*The Green Box: A Book of Dreams*). Vienna: Paul Zsolnay Verlag, 2007.

Platonov tajni roman: Platonov gradoslovni nauk (*Plato's Secret Novel: Plato's Lessons on the City*). Novi Sad, Serbia: Mediterran Publishing, 2008.

Acknowledgments

Several organizations helped me publish Bogdan Bogdanović's little-known photographs. This book would not have been possible without the financial support provided by the Graham Foundation for Advanced Studies in the Fine Arts. Equally critical was the generous assistance of the Architekturzentrum Wien, which holds Bogdan Bogdanović's archive and graciously permitted us to reproduce his photographs at the heart of this project. I am especially grateful to AzW's Monika Platzer and Iris Ranzinger for their enthusiasm and understanding. A fellowship at the Center for Advanced Study in the Visual Arts at the National Gallery of Art in Washington, D.C., in the summer of 2015 allowed me to begin my research into Bogdanović's intellectual formation. Membership at the Institute for Advanced Study in Princeton in fall 2017 afforded me the time to write.

I owe special thanks to Wolfgang Thaler, who was involved in developing the idea for this book from the very beginning. He assisted in making the initial selection of images, and he also enlisted the aid of Tobias Urban, who kindly allowed us to use his scanning equipment to digitize the photos. Jelica Jovanović invested countless hours carefully scanning the slides and researching Bogdanović's archive.

Many thanks to everyone at The Museum of Modern Art whose efforts brought this volume to fruition. Martino Stierli, the Philip Johnson Chief Curator of Architecture and Design, generously provided support at a critical juncture in the project's development. Christopher Hudson, the Museum's Publisher, went out of his way to ensure its realization. Anna Kats's advice was much appreciated. Producing a book can be a long and tedious process; not in this case—everyone involved made it a pleasure. Don McMahon's editorial input was invaluable. Prudence Peiffer was a generous editor who helped make the words flow. Matthew Pimm made the images shine. And last but not least, Amanda Washburn gave the book its final shape through her imaginative design. My sincere thanks to all.

In many ways, this book owes its existence to the enthusiasm and support of Ksenija Anastasijević Bogdanović, who sadly did not live to see it in print. I dedicate the book to her memory.

VLADIMIR KULIĆ

Generous support for this publication is provided by the Graham Foundation for Advanced Studies in the Fine Arts.

Produced by the Department of Publications, The Museum of Modern Art, New York
Christopher Hudson, Publisher
Don McMahon, Editorial Director
Marc Sapir, Production Director

Edited by Prudence Peiffer
Designed by Amanda Washburn
Production by Matthew Pimm
Printed and bound by Livonia Print, Riga

This book is typeset in Nuber. The paper is 150 gsm Magnosatin.

Published by The Museum of Modern Art
11 West 53 Street
New York, NY 10019-5497
www.moma.org

The interview with Bogdan Bogdanović and all quotations of Bogdanović were translated from Serbo-Croatian by Vladimir Kulić.

Library of Congress Control Number: 2018936431
ISBN: 978-1-63345-052-3

Distributed in the United States and Canada by
ARTBOOK | D.A.P.
75 Broad Street, Suite 630
New York, NY 10004
www.artbook.com

Distributed outside the United States and Canada by
Thames & Hudson Ltd
181A High Holborn
London WC1V 7QX
www.thamesandhudson.com

Front cover: Jasenovac Memorial Site, Jasenovac, Croatia. 1959–66. Bogdan Bogdanović (1922–2010). Architekturzentrum Wien, Collection. Photograph by Bogdan Bogdanović

Back cover: Slobodište Memorial Park, Kruševac, Serbia. 1960–65. Bogdan Bogdanović (1922–2010). Architekturzentrum Wien, Collection. Photograph by Bogdan Bogdanović

P. 2: Necropolis for the Victims of Fascism, Novi Travnik, Bosnia and Herzegovina. 1971–75. Bogdan Bogdanović (1922–2010). Architekturzentrum Wien, Collection. Photograph by Bogdan Bogdanović

P. 4: Garavice Memorial Park, Bihać, Bosnia and Herzegovina. 1969–81. Bogdan Bogdanović (1922–2010). Architekturzentrum Wien, Collection. Photograph by Bogdan Bogdanović

P. 6: Mausoleum of Struggle and Victory, Čačak, Serbia. 1970–80. Bogdan Bogdanović (1922–2010). Architekturzentrum Wien, Collection. Photograph by Bogdan Bogdanović

Printed and bound in Latvia